This Book Belongs To:

____

____

____

Published by Anglican House Media Ministry, Inc., Newport Beach, California. You may contact us online at www.anglicanhousemedia.org. Printed by Asia Printing Co., Ltd., Seoul, Korea. Text set in Baskerville typeface.

Anglican House
Media Ministry

ISBN 978-0-9970167-2-7

The Nicene Creed

Illustrated and Instructed

For Kids

For my wife.

I love you Brandie with all of my heart. Thank you for standing with me through it all.

To my children Sam, Jack, Luke, and Lila:

Let this amazing faith, handed down from generation to generation, lead you to your Heavenly Father's outstretched arms. I am proud to be your Dad.

CONTENTS

PAGE

About The Author

Photo by Holly Bracy

Joey Fitzgerald is a priest in the Anglican Church of North America and is the Rector of the Church of the Outer Banks in Nags Head, NC. He and his wife Brandie are the parents of four children: Sam, Jack, Luke, and Lila. Before he was ordained, Joey taught art in public schools. He enjoys using art as a tool in sharing the Gospel of Jesus.

Dear Reader,

For over 1600 years the Nicene Creed has been the standard of orthodoxy across Christian traditions. It anchors our faith by stating the essential beliefs of Christianity. Written in 325 A.D. at the Council of Nicea, and finalized in 381 A.D. at the Council of Constantinople, the Creed corrected a heresy that denied the divinity of Jesus Christ. The deception that Jesus Christ is not God, but only a good man, lives on today in many who profess to follow Christ. By believing and reciting the Scriptural truths found in the words of the Creed, we safeguard ourselves from false beliefs that lead us away from God.

It is our responsibility to teach God's truths to our children. They are full members of the church too, and they deserve to know the good news of the Gospel. That is why God says of his words:

> "Make them known to your children and your children's children."
> DEUTERONOMY 4:9

The Nicene Creed truly is a remarkable document! It is deeply faithful to Holy Scripture, God's Word; succinct, yet fully expressive of the Christian faith. It unifies us in the midst of today's individualistic culture. It is an act of heart-forming worship of the One True God. As we say the Nicene Creed, we are reminded that God is Triune: One God, but *three persons*. The Father is glorified, Christ is exalted, and the Holy Spirit is invited.

My hope and prayer is that this book for the edification of children will be the first step in a new generation's unpacking the treasures of God's Truth. Read it with your children, talk about it. There are scripture references throughout, so you can grab a Bible and dig in further if you like.

This is our faith. I hope that you hand it down!

Peace and Blessings,
Rev. Joey Fitzgerald

A Note on the Christian Creeds

The Creeds acknowledged in Christendom are the Athanasian Creed, the Apostles' Creed, and the Nicene Creed. Of these the most widely used is the Nicene Creed.

What is a creed?

A creed is a statement of faith. The word "creed" comes from the Latin credo, meaning "I believe." JOHN 20:24-29

What is the purpose of the Creeds?

The purpose of the Creeds is to declare and safeguard God's truth about himself, about ourselves, and about creation, as God has revealed it in Holy Scripture. 2 PETER 1:19-2; JOHN 20:31

What does belief in the Creeds signify?

Belief in the Creeds signifies acceptance of God's revealed truth, and the intention to live by it. 2 TIMOTHY 3:14-15

Why do Christians acknowledge these creeds?

You acknowledge them together with the Church because they are grounded in Holy Scripture and are faithful expressions of its teaching. 1 CORINTHIANS 15:3-11; PHILIPPIANS 2:6-11

Why should you know these Creeds?

You should know these Creeds because they state the essential beliefs of the Christian faith.

Note: These questions and answers are taken from: *To Be A Christian: An Anglican Catechism.* Anglican House Publishers, 2014. ISBN 978-0-9860441-2-0

Why Share the Creed with Children?

You might be asking yourself why you should take the time to teach children about The Nicene Creed. Is it really that important?

The answer is absolutely yes! The Nicene Creed states the essence of God's truths, as revealed in Holy Scripture. And Holy Scripture makes it perfectly clear that young children are to be taught the truths of God:

> "the Lord said to me, 'Gather the people to me, that I may let them hear my words, so that they may learn to fear me all the days that they live on the earth, and that they may teach their children so.'" DEUTERONOMY 4:10

> "You shall teach them to your children, talking of them when you are sitting in your house, and when you are walking by the way, and when you lie down, and when you rise." DEUTERONOMY 11:19

Even the youngest child has an inborn longing to connect with God's truths, which are fully revealed in Jesus Christ. And Jesus certainly wants to connect with each child:

> " Now they were bringing even infants to him that he might touch them. And when the disciples saw it, they rebuked them. But Jesus called them to him, saying, "Let the children come to me, and do not hinder them, for to such belongs the kingdom of God. Truly, I say to you, whoever does not receive the kingdom of God like a child shall not enter it." LUKE 18:15-17

There are many promises connected with the Lord's admonitions, and this particular promise concerning children is perfectly clear:

> "Train up a child in the way he should go; even when he is old he will not depart from it." PROVERBS 22:6

When we are teaching God's truths, children will ask amazingly penetrating and powerful questions! With this in mind, we have included **Keywords For Kids**. It's a glossary of word meanings for children, together with one or more examples for each word. (It's a pretty good idea to have a good look at it before using the book with your children or students!)

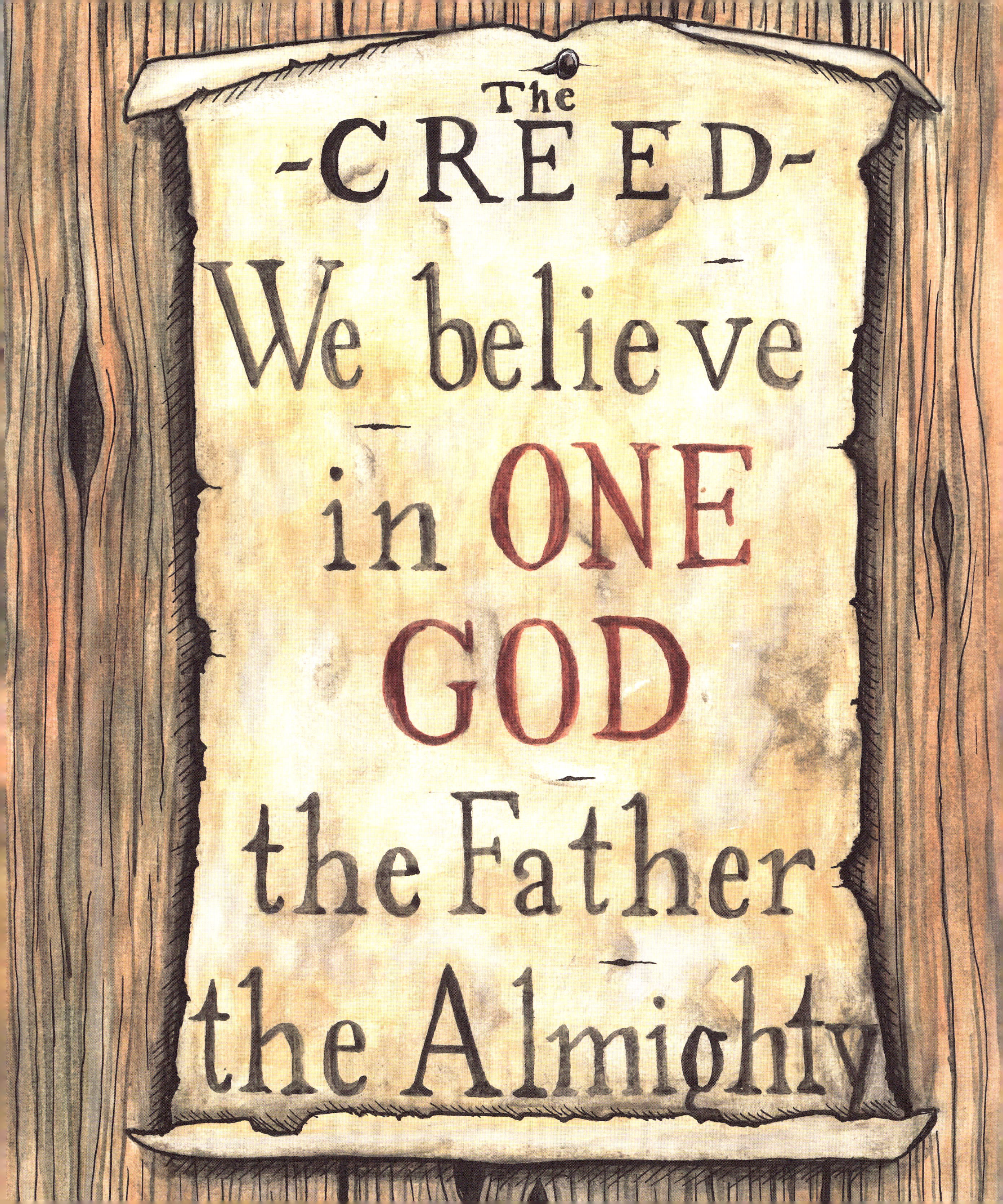

The
-CREED-

We believe
in ONE
GOD
the Father
the Almighty

We believe in one God, the Father, the Almighty, maker of heaven and earth, of all that is, visible and invisible.

God is completely unique. There has never been anyone like him, and there never will be! ISAIAH 45:5-6 God does not have a beginning, and he does not have an end. PSALM 90:2 God is the Creator of everything that exists. He made things we can see, like the sun, the moon, and the stars. He made chickens, llamas, cucumbers, baby sisters, and bananas. He even created the things we can't see, like music, our thought, angels, Heaven, and our spirits. GENESIS 1

God loves all of his creation very much! However, it is his people that he loves the most. He lovingly made you and all people. He created us in his image and wants us to be his children. That is why we call him "Father." GENESIS 2; GALATIONS 4:4-7

We believe in one Lord, Jesus Christ,
the only Son of God,
eternally begotten of the Father,
God from God, Light from Light,
true God from true God,
begotten, not made,
of one Being with the Father,
through him all things were made.

Jesus is the Son of the Father. MATTHEW 3:17 This doesn't mean that God the Father created Jesus. There was never a time when Jesus was not there! When the Father was dreaming about the world he wanted to make, Jesus was dreaming with him. JOHN 1:1-5 Before they made you they thought about every single little detail. They knew what color of hair they wanted you to have, what color of skin; if you would be tall or short, big or small. And they loved you then as much as they do now.

When the Nicene Creed says that Jesus Christ is "Light from Light" and "True God from True God," it means that Jesus and the Father are both God. Jesus is not just the *son* of God, he is God *the Son*. It is because the Father and the Son love the world so much that God the Son came to Earth.

For us and for our salvation he came down from heaven, was incarnate from the Holy Spirit and the Virgin Mary, and was made man.

The Incarnation is a fancy way of saying that God the Son became a human too. He was born as a baby, just like you. His earthly parents Mary and Joseph named him Jesus. LUKE 2:1-21 He had skin, hair, arms, legs, fingers and toes! He learned to walk and talk, and to read and write. He played with friends, swam in rivers, helped Joseph work as a carpenter, learned in the synagogue, and grew up to be an amazing person! LUKE 2:41-52 Jesus is all God and he is all man! LUKE 24:39, PHILIPIANS 3:21

Why was it so important for God the Son to become a human being and come to Earth? When God made the first people, Adam and Eve, they disobeyed him. GENESIS 3 Disobeying God is called sin, and no one is free from it. ROMANS 3:23 We have all disobeyed God in our own way. Sin keeps us away from God. God is the creator of all life. If we are separated from him, we can't have the life that he wants for us on Earth or forever with him in Heaven. God wants us to be with him and to have life! This is why Jesus came; to forgive us our sins, to give us life, and to rescue the whole world. ROMANS 6:23 This is called salvation, and it is a free gift that God gives to all who believe in him! ROMANS 1:16

For our sake he was crucified
under Pontius Pilate;
he suffered death and was buried.
On the third day he rose again
in accordance with the Scriptures;

Salvation comes to us because Jesus is both a man and God! When he died on the cross, he took away our sins. 1PETER 2:24 Jesus' friends were sad and afraid. They didn't understand what Jesus had to do. They hid in a room from Friday until Sunday. JOHN 20:19 That's when something really amazing happened…

Jesus rose from the grave! We call this the ressurection. He was there, with the apostles, the other disciples, and family, fully alive! 1CORINTHIANS 15:3-8 People from all over Israel saw him. He spoke to them, walked with them, and even sat down at a table and ate food with them.

When Jesus died and rose again, he defeated death completely. Now you and I, and anyone who follows him, can live forever with God! JOHN 3:16 And we don't even have to wait until we get to Heaven to experience his power and love. It begins now, as soon as we start to follow him! JOHN 10:10

He ascended into heaven
and is seated at the right hand of the Father.
He will come again in glory to judge the
living and the dead,
and his kingdom will have no end.

After Jesus rose, he spent time with his followers. He told them that he was going to go be with the Father, and he would send them a helper, God the Holy Spirit. After that, Jesus went up into Heaven to be with the Father. ACTS 1:1-11

Jesus promised that he would come back one day, but that only God the Father knows the day and the hour. MARK 13:32 When Jesus comes back, the Kingdom of God will be complete! We will have a new Heaven and a new Earth that will come together into one wonderful world! God's Kingdom is totally perfect. There will be no tears, no pain, and no death, and God's people will experience real, unending life! REVELATION 21:1-4

is not
THE FATHER
THE SON
is
is
GOD
is not
is not
is
THE HOLY SPIRIT

We believe in the Holy Spirit, the Lord,
the giver of life,
who proceeds from the Father
[and the Son],

We have already said that the Father and the Son are both God. Even though there is only One God, he is made up of three separate persons. This is called the Trinity. The Holy Spirit is the third person of God. JOHN 14:26

This can be really confusing. Sometimes pictures can help us to better understand complicated ideas. The picture on the opposite page is called the Shield of the Trinity. Christians a long time ago drew pictures like this to help them understand how God could be three persons in One God.

Look at the symbol for the Holy Spirit. The symbol is a dove. Do you remember the story of when the Holy Spirit descended like a dove on Jesus? MATTHEW 3:16 Follow the line from the dove to the middle. The Holy Spirit is God! If you follow the circle around, you will see that the Holy Spirit is not the Father, and he is not the Son. However, together, all three make the One True God. The fullness of God is in each person of the Holy Trinity.

Each member of the Trinity has a unique role. The Holy Spirit's job is to comfort us, and remind us to always look to Jesus as our Lord. The Holy Spirit fills us with God's power. In the Holy Spirit we are joined to God and to other Christians! JOHN 16:7-15, EPHESIANS 4:4

Who with the Father and the Son is worshiped and glorified, who has spoken through the prophets.

The Holy Spirit has always been with the Father and the Son, and he helped the Father and the Son to create our universe. GENESIS 1:1-2 Through the Holy Spirit, God has spoken to the world through his people, Scripture, and the Church. Before Jesus died, rose, and ascended into Heaven, the Holy Spirit only came to a few people and at special times. Now, the Holy Spirit has been poured out and he is at work around us everyday. ACTS 2:17, JOHN 15:26, JOHN 16 7-15 As you will find out, the Holy Spirit can work through you, too!

Jesus said that if we have faith in him, we can experience the power of his Kingdom now, even doing the same things that Jesus did. JOHN 14:12-14 We can do that because the Holy Spirit fills us with love, joy, peace, patience, kindness, goodness, faithfulness, gentleness, and self-control, and all sorts of other good gifts. GALATIONS 5:22-23, 1 CORINTHIANS 12:8-10 He does this to help us be more like Jesus and to faithfully serve the Kingdom of God!

We believe in one holy catholic and apostolic Church. We acknowledge one baptism for the forgiveness of sins.

Jesus told his followers they would receive power when the Holy Spirit came. After Jesus returned to Heaven to be with the Father, the Holy Spirit came upon the Apostles, and many of Jesus' other followers, just as Jesus promised. ACTS 1:8, 2:1-4 Immediately, they began to tell other people about his death, resurrection, and the love of the Father! These people became the first Church. The Church includes all the people who have ever followed Jesus, and all those who will follow him in the future, no matter where, or when they live! MATTHEW 28:19

Baptism shows that we are united with Christ in his death and in his resurrection. ROMANS 6:1-11 Jesus was baptized by John the Baptist, and Jesus commanded his followers to baptize others in the name of the Father and of the Son and of the Holy Spirit. MATTHEW 3:1-17, 28:19-20 When we are baptized, we confess that we will follow Jesus and we reject Satan and all evil things. We also confess that we believe all that the Bible teaches, and that we will be obedient to God's teaching and commandments.

We look for the resurrection of the dead, and the life of the world to come. Amen.

One day, this world will end, but our lives will go on forever in God's Kingdom of the new Heaven and new Earth. All those who have become adopted children of God, through Jesus, will live in this new world, and it will never, ever end! There will be feasts, parties, friends, families, angels, and so much more! REVELATION 21 Best of all, God will be with us, Father, Son, and Holy Spirit!

When we follow Jesus, these are the things we agree to believe. It is not always easy, but through God's grace, we can choose to follow him even when it is hard. This is called faith, and, when we have faith in God, he will never leave us!

Are you ready to believe the words of the Nicene Creed and to have faith?

Are you ready to experience the love of God, starting right now?

Whenever you are ready, you can close your eyes, and say a prayer like this:

"Dear God, I believe in Jesus Christ. I want to give my life to him, and experience the love of the Father, the grace of the Son, and have the Holy Spirit fill me with his peace."

Life of the Wor

to come.

The Nice

We believe in one God,
the Father, the Almighty,
maker of heaven and earth,
of all that is, visible and invisible.

We believe in one Lord, Jesus Christ,
the only Son of God,
eternally begotten of the Father,
God from God, Light from Light,
true God from true God,
begotten, not made,
of one Being with the Father;
through him all things were made.
For us and for our salvation he came down from heaven,
was incarnate from the Holy Spirit and the Virgin Mary,
and was made man.
For our sake he was crucified under Pontius Pilate;
he suffered death and was buried.
On the third day he rose again in accordance with the Scriptures;
He ascended into heaven
and is seated at the right hand of the Father.
He will come again in glory to judge the living and the dead,
and his kingdom will have no end.

ne Creed

We believe in the Holy Spirit, the Lord, the giver of life,
who proceeds from the Father [and the Son].
who with the Father and the Son is worshiped and
glorified, who has spoken through the prophets.
We believe in one holy catholic and apostolic Church.
We acknowledge one baptism for the forgiveness of sins.
We look for the resurrection of the dead,
and the life of the world to come. Amen.

Note: 1. Some traditions use the singular *I Believe* rather than the plural *We Believe*.
2. The phrase known as the *filioque* [and the Son] is not in the original Greek text. Nevertheless, in the Western Church, the *filioque* [and the Son] is customary in worship.

Keywords for Kids

Word	Meaning	Example(s)
Almighty	Able to do things that no one else can do	Only God is all powerful!
Amen	To agree with something	Jesus loves you! Amen!
Apostles	Jesus' closest 12 disciples	Peter, Andrew, James, John, Philip, Bartholomew, Simon, Thomas, Thaddaeus, James, Matthew, and Judas. Later, Paul became an apostle too!
Apostolic	What the Apostles learned from Jesus and taught others.	Some of the apostles wrote most of the books and letters of the New Testament.
Ascension	Going up	A balloon can ascend (go up) in the sky.
Baptism	Being presented to Jesus and adopted into God's Family.	Jesus was baptized in water by John the Baptist in the Jordan River.
Begotten	Having a daddy	Jesus' daddy is God the Father.
Believe	Trusting that what we know is really true	We trust and know that Jesus loves us very much!
Catholic	Something that is all around the world	Jesus' church is all over the world.
Christ	Jesus' title and job	Jesus is the Christ, the savior of the world!

Keywords for Kids

Word	Meaning	Example(s)
Creed	Words that describe what we believe	We believe that Jesus died for our sins and opens Heaven to all who believe.
Crucified	Killed on a cross	Long ago, Roman soldiers would crucify criminals.
Eternal	No beginning and no end, for ever and ever	God is eternal and we will live with him in Heaven for ever and ever!
Forgiveness	Letting go of feelings that have been hurt	We forgive someone when we let go of our hurt feelings and just love them.
Glorified	Lifted up and placed where all can see	A trophy is placed on shelf so that everyone can see it.
Grace	God's favor to us, free and undeserved	Grace is the means by which we receive God's loving care for us.
God	The Creator of the World, who has always been and will always be	God has three persons: God the Father, God the Son, and God the Holy Spirit.
Gospel	Good news	The God news of Jesus as told in the Bible, specifically in Matthew, Mark, Luke, and John.

Keywords for Kids

Word	Meaning	Example(s)
Heaven	God's home	Even though we can't see it, it is just as real as where you are, only better!
Holy	Made his own by God	We are made Holy because God has adopted us as his children.
Holy Spirit	He is theThird Person of the Trinity	The Holy Spirit helps us to love others and he turns our hearts to Jesus.
Incarnate	Having a real body	When Jesus came to earth, he had a real body with skin, hair and everything!
Invisible	Something that can't be looked at with our eyes	The wind, our thoughts, and music are all unseen, but very real.
Jesus	The second Person of the Trinity	Jesus is God, the Son of the Father.
Kingdom	The land and people that a king is ruler of	God's Kingdom is in Heaven and on Earth.
Pontius Pilate	A Roman ruler who lived in Israel	Pontius Pilate was in charge of Jesus' trial and ordered his death on the Cross.
Prophets	People that speak God's words to others.	Isaiah and John the Baptist were two of the prophets.

Keywords for Kids

Word	Meaning	Example(s)
Resurrection	Coming back to life after death	Jesus came back to life and prepares a place for us in His Kingdom for the day we are resurrected to new life!
Salvation	To be saved from something	We are saved, by Jesus, from eternal death!
Satan	The enemy who would lead us away from God	Satan wants us to ignore God.
Scriptures	The words of God in the Bible	Genesis, Psalms, and The Gospel of John are some books of the Bible
Sin	The things that keep us from God	When we disobey God and his desire for our lives.
Spirits	The invisible part of who we are.	In Heaven, God gives us new bodies for our spirits to live in.
Trinity	Three persons in One	God has three persons; Father, Son, and Holy Spirit, but he is ONE God.
Virgin Mary	Jesus' earthly mother	Mary had Jesus by a miracle of the Holy Spirit.
Worship	Giving love to God	We worship God when we show him love by singing, praying, and obeying him.